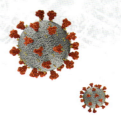

MEDIA AND COMMUNICATIONS DURING COVID-19

BY CAROL HAND

CONTENT CONSULTANT
Hans Schmidt, PhD
Associate Professor of Communications
Coordinator, Schreyer and Cooper Honors Programs
Penn State University Brandywine

Essential Library

An Imprint of Abdo Publishing
abdobooks.com

ABDOBOOKS.COM

Published by Abdo Publishing, a division of ABDO, PO Box 398166, Minneapolis, Minnesota 55439. Copyright © 2023 by Abdo Consulting Group, Inc. International copyrights reserved in all countries. No part of this book may be reproduced in any form without written permission from the publisher. Essential Library™ is a trademark and logo of Abdo Publishing.

Printed in the United States of America, North Mankato, Minnesota.
052022
092022

THIS BOOK CONTAINS RECYCLED MATERIALS

Cover Photo: Kate Kultsevych/Shutterstock Images
Interior Photos: Eye Press/Newscom, 4; Ren Yong/Imagine China/AP Images, 8; Salvatore Di Nolfi/Keystone/AP Images, 12; Dake Kang/AP Images, 16; Yasushi Kanno/The Yomiuri Shimbun/AP Images, 19; Shutterstock Images, 23, 38, 42; Red Line Editorial, 24, 30; Ted S. Warren/AP Images, 26; Adam Calaitzis/Shutterstock Images, 32; Prostock Studio/Shutterstock Images, 37; Vasin Lee/Shutterstock Images, 46; Ben Hasty/MediaNews Group/Reading Eagle/Getty Images, 50; Jan Woitas/Picture Alliance/DPA/AP Images, 56; Chip Somodevilla/Getty Images News/Getty Images, 58, 99; Saul Loeb/AFP/Getty Images, 60; Pat Nabong/Chicago Sun-Times/AP Images, 63; Eric Lee/Bloomberg/Getty Images, 67; Hans Pennink/Shutterstock Images, 70; Jessica Girvan/Shutterstock Images, 73; Frederic J. Brown/AFP/Getty Images, 78; Alex Brandon/AP Images, 82; Olga Ganovicheva/Shutterstock Images, 86; Britta Pedersen/Picture Alliance/DPA/AP Images, 89; Glyn Kirk/AFP/Getty Images, 92; Caroline Brehman/CQ Roll Call/AP Images, 95

Editor: Marie Pearson
Designer: Becky Daum

Library of Congress Control Number: 2021951382
Publisher's Cataloging-in-Publication Data
Names: Hand, Carol, author.
Title: Media and communications during covid-19 / by Carol Hand
Description: Minneapolis, Minnesota : Abdo Publishing, 2023 | Series: Fighting covid-19 | Includes online resources and index.
Identifiers: ISBN 9781532197987 (lib. bdg.) | ISBN 9781098271633 (ebook)
Subjects: LCSH: COVID-19 (Disease)--Juvenile literature. | Social media--Juvenile literature. | Distance education--Juvenile literature. | COVID-19 (Disease) in mass media--Juvenile literature. | Videoconferencing--Juvenile literature. | Civilization, Modern--21st century--Juvenile literature. | United States--History--Juvenile literature.
Classification: DDC 614.592--dc23

CONTENTS

CHAPTER ONE
THE COVID-19 STORY
4

CHAPTER TWO
EARLY INFORMATION
16

CHAPTER THREE
THE MAINSTREAM MEDIA
26

CHAPTER FOUR
SOCIAL MEDIA
38

CHAPTER FIVE
HOW MEDIA USE CHANGED
50

CHAPTER SIX
THE INTRODUCTION OF COVID-19 VACCINES
60

CHAPTER SEVEN
MEDIA BIAS
70

CHAPTER EIGHT
FROM PANDEMIC TO PART OF LIFE
82

CHAPTER NINE
ANTICIPATING THE NEXT PANDEMIC
92

ESSENTIAL FACTS	100	INDEX	110
GLOSSARY	102	ABOUT THE AUTHOR	112
ADDITIONAL RESOURCES	104	ABOUT THE CONSULTANT	112
SOURCE NOTES	106		

CHAPTER ONE

THE COVID-19 STORY

In January 2020, the global media was only gradually becoming aware that the world was about to plunge into a deadly pandemic. *Media* refers to the many ways in which people communicate information to a large population. It includes everything from individual social media users to large international news agencies.

When an infectious virus first arose in Wuhan, China, in early December 2019, the Chinese government strictly controlled news about it. Thus, the public was unaware of the potential danger. During December, a Chinese lab misidentified the virus as the severe acute respiratory syndrome (SARS) coronavirus, which had caused an epidemic from 2002 to 2004. On December 30, an ophthalmologist named Li Wenliang, who worked in the hospital that had requested the lab tests of the virus, shared information about the supposed SARS outbreak with his students. He warned them, "Don't circulate the

Ophthalmologist Li Wenliang was one of the first people to alert others about a virus spreading in Wuhan, China.

5

message outside this group. Get your family and loved ones to take precautions."[1] But others shared screenshots of Li's message on social media, and soon millions of people across China knew about the virus.

Epidemiologist Marjorie Pollack, deputy editor of the Program for Monitoring Emerging Diseases (ProMED-mail), became concerned about the virus after a colleague in Taiwan emailed her. Pollack had alerted the world to SARS in 2003, and now, even without confirmation from the Chinese government, she felt the virus again posed a threat. She emailed her 80,000 subscribers on December 30, sharing news of the virus spreading in China to the Western world. Although international law states that the World Health Organization (WHO) must be informed of a potentially dangerous disease outbreak within 24 hours of its appearance, the Chinese government had still made no official report. It only said the virus was under control and there was no evidence of human-to-human transmission. By December 31, Chinese scientists had identified it as a new virus. However, George Gao, director general of the Chinese Center for Disease Control and Prevention, stated privately to Ian Lipkin, a Columbia University epidemiologist, that the virus was not highly transmissible. Later, Gao insisted he never said publicly that there was no transmission between humans.

The WHO meetings that began on January 1, 2020, were at first based on vague reports and social media posts. Chinese state-run media reported the country's first death from the virus on January 11, 2020. Not until January 20 did state media confirm the virus's human-to-human transmission.

Starting on January 2, the Chinese state media had begun a campaign to prevent doctors from sharing their concerns about the virus. It described these doctors as "rumour mongers" and "internet users."[2] It brought them in for questioning, saying it did this to prevent doctors from spreading unconfirmed information. Li, whose warning to his students had gone viral, was forced to

PROMED-MAIL

ProMED-mail, or the Program for Monitoring Emerging Diseases, serves as an early warning system for detecting and reporting disease outbreaks around the world. It collects reports of any disease that affects humans, whether infectious or toxic in nature, and whether naturally or intentionally released. ProMED-mail is open to everyone free of charge and does not claim any political influence. It carefully screens disease reports for validity. Reports are judged by a panel of experts and then posted on the internet and emailed to subscribers in more than 150 countries. Marjorie Pollack used this service to raise awareness of the new virus that led to the COVID-19 pandemic.

Although Chinese media had been reporting on the virus, few people realized how big a threat it posed at first. People continued to gather in Wuhan on January 14, as they traveled for Lunar New Year celebrations.

sign a confession that his warning was untrue. Li died of the virus on February 7, 2020. His death led to a social media backlash against the Chinese government, citing its mishandling of the coronavirus crisis and online censorship. Four days later, the International Committee on Taxonomy of Viruses named the virus severe acute respiratory syndrome coronavirus 2 (SARS-CoV-2). The WHO named its resulting disease COVID-19.

The British Broadcasting Corporation (BBC) tried several times during January to obtain interviews about the virus with the Chinese government and the head of the Chinese Center for Disease Control and Prevention.

It was turned down. CNN was one of the earliest US media outlets to cover the development of the pandemic. It published an article about the "mysterious virus" on January 7 and multiple articles thereafter.[3] Some other US outlets published stories in early January too.

EARLY COVERAGE

In the beginning, the virus spread much faster than the media coverage describing it. The viral threat seemed distant, and news coverage was sparse. But then on January 21, the United States had its first confirmed case of the virus. As case numbers and deaths began to climb, news coverage increased. By the end of the first 100 days, on April 9, 2020, COVID-19 had become the biggest US news story.

According to a September 2020 report by Project Information Literacy, the early coverage of the coronavirus

> "Borders are closed, aircraft grounded and ships anchored as WHO mutely dithers [hesitates] over whether or not to declare an emergency."[4]
>
> —Amir Attaran, professor of law and epidemiology at the University of Ottawa (Canada) and critic of the WHO

story occurred in three waves. The first wave was slow and lasted through January. During this time, the virus was mostly confined to China, and the Chinese government was doing its best to keep the virus and the story contained. But new cases were soon identified in Taiwan, Japan, Thailand, and South Korea, as well as in the United States. On January 30, the WHO declared COVID-19 a global health emergency.

Because the virus spread rapidly and was highly contagious, containment soon became impossible. A steep rise in news coverage marked the beginning of the second wave, which lasted from February 1 through March 10. On February 11, the WHO officially gave the disease the name COVID-19, short for coronavirus disease 2019. The United States reported its first death on February 29 in Seattle,

A HEALTH EMERGENCY

The WHO declared a global health emergency on January 30, 2020. This occurred after the new coronavirus outbreak had spread to several countries outside China and exhibited human-to-human transmission. The WHO declarations provide guidance but are not backed up by law. Individual governments choose how to respond to an emergency. The WHO's declaration indicated the seriousness of the situation, although some people thought it should have spoken out earlier.

Washington, although it was later confirmed that two earlier deaths had occurred in California. During this time, deaths were reported around the world, from Asia to Europe to North and South America.

On March 11, 2020, the WHO officially declared COVID-19 a global pandemic, initiating the third wave of media coverage, which lasted through April 9. The day after this declaration, the pandemic was front-page news and would remain so for the rest of the year. This news coverage raised people's concern about the dangers of the virus, influencing nearly every area of life. It impacted economies, causing the stock market to plummet. It triggered the cancellation of major sporting events, including part of the 2019–2020 National Basketball Association (NBA) season.

The pandemic had begun, and the world was a different place. Countries reacted differently. The United States began to urge state and local governments and organizations to cancel gatherings or limit their sizes. In the last week of January, various countries, including the United States, began to screen all airline travelers from China. Tech companies shut down their offices in China, Hong Kong, and Taiwan. The European Union banned all

WHO director general Tedros Adhanom Ghebreyesus held press conferences that gave the media information about developments in research on the new virus.

travelers from other nations. The news media scrambled to keep pace with the rapid changes occurring in society.

MIDDLE AND LATE COVID-19 COVERAGE

As the disease spread, media coverage expanded its scope to include not only the pandemic but also the reactions of governments and health agencies. All early information on the virus itself was tentative, but case numbers and deaths were clearly rising. Headlines told people to stay at home, avoid crowded places, and keep their kids home from school to do distance learning. They described shortages of the testing kits and ventilators needed to help the sick, and shortages of personal protective equipment needed to keep caregivers safe.

Throughout the pandemic, people in the media criticized various individuals and agencies for how they handled the pandemic. They criticized agencies such as the US Centers for Disease Control and Prevention (CDC) for being unprepared, reacting slowly, and giving conflicting advice. A CDC official warned early on that the virus would begin spreading through the population, but it was weeks before the CDC officially recommended that people stop gathering in groups. And after saying for months that healthy people need not wear masks, it later reversed this recommendation. During this confusing time, the media contributed to the confusion by repeating the muddled and sometimes incorrect information it received from

> "One thing that science journalists have been getting better at is not just saying what we do know, but what we don't know. But most journalists aren't accustomed to doing that."[5]
>
> —Laura Helmuth, editor-in-chief of Scientific American

WHAT IS GOOD MEDIA COVERAGE?

High scientific quality and low sensationalism are important to good media coverage of a pandemic. Poor science coverage may overstate or understate disease risks, fail to properly describe protective measures, or poorly explain evidence. This makes it difficult for individuals to make health decisions and for policy makers to determine government actions. It may put health professionals at greater risk for disease. Sensationalized or false media information may increase disease risks and make it more difficult to control a pandemic. Good media coverage also uses reliable expert sources. Peer-reviewed medical journals and local, state, and federal health departments are examples of good sources for articles about COVID-19.

the CDC and other official sources.

Media coverage has depended on information released by official sources. Coverage can be only as good as the information available. At the beginning, when COVID-19 was new, information was scarce and conflicting, and the media learned along with disease specialists. As scientists learned more about the disease, media sources could provide information that was more correct and more useful. In the meantime, reporters had to learn to tell the public what they didn't know, as well as what they did. Good reporting also relied on members of the media knowing which people and organizations were valid, trustworthy sources.

COVID-19 COVERAGE PRE- AND POSTVACCINE

Throughout 2020, as the pandemic worsened, case numbers and deaths soared in the United States and around the world. A new phase in pandemic media coverage occurred with the search for a COVID-19 vaccine. Some clinical trials began in March 2020. The first COVID-19 vaccine was released in December 2020. By November 9, 2021, 57.3 percent of Americans were fully vaccinated.[6] Some people were hesitant or unwilling to get vaccinated. People on all sides expressed their opinions on social media.

At the end of 2021, almost two years after the pandemic began, news coverage was much less intense, and life seemingly was returning to a new and slightly different form of normal than before COVID-19. But the virus continued to circulate throughout society. And the COVID-19 experience has probably forever changed the way the news media—both traditional and social—will cover future pandemics.

CHAPTER TWO

EARLY INFORMATION

US media coverage on the COVID-19 pandemic got off to a slow start. But the US military, specifically the Defense Intelligence Agency (DIA), knew about the virus and its potential dangers as early as November 2019. The DIA's National Center for Medical Intelligence produced a report based on analysis of wire and computer intercepts and satellite images from China. It warned of dangers to the US military in Asia and a potential "cataclysmic event" that could reach US shores.[1] The report was seen by the DIA, the Pentagon's Joint Staff, and the White House. Information from the report was included in the president's daily intelligence briefing in early January, by which time it had been thoroughly analyzed and verified.

But in public, word of the possible pandemic had spread slowly, and various individuals and groups did not identify it as a concern. President Donald Trump first

Early news coverage of the new virus was sparse, but a few articles gave updates about Wuhan, such as the use of temperature guns to make sure people did not have fevers.

TO MASK OR NOT TO MASK?

Early in the pandemic, the CDC and the WHO said a mask was necessary only if you were sick or were caring for a person with COVID-19. But on April 3, 2020, the CDC changed its guidelines, recommending that everyone wear a face mask to protect against COVID-19. The WHO did not match this recommendation. This disagreement led to mistrust of the agencies. But the WHO's guidelines were meant for the entire world. National Foundation for Infectious Diseases medical director William Schaffner suggested that the reason the WHO did not update its recommendation was that in many regions, masks were unavailable. Insisting on their use would be impractical for the WHO. Also, mask wearing by everyone could result in masks being unavailable for health-care workers, who needed them most.

commented on the virus on January 22. When asked if he was worried about a pandemic, he said, "Not at all. And we have it totally under control."[2] However, on January 31, he restricted air travel to and from China.

A number of infectious disease specialists, including some from Harvard Medical School, also stated in January 2020 that people should be more concerned about the flu. Much of this early lack of concern stemmed from lack of knowledge. The CDC, the WHO, and other public health officials were inconsistent or slow in their recommendations on wearing masks, avoiding groups, and other mitigating factors. The traditional media contributed to the confusion

Although many people in countries such as Japan were buying masks to protect themselves from the virus, countries such as the United States did not recommend masks at first.

by repeating the conflicting information given by these sources.

But neither the experts nor the journalists really knew what was going on. The virus was completely new, little was known about it, and that knowledge changed daily as new evidence emerged. Journalist Peter Kafka said that the media dropped the ball on COVID-19. In the future, he said, it should do a better job of keeping the public updated without panicking them as the level of knowledge changes. The best solution, Kafka said, is probably to say, "The experts we talked to aren't sure, but they're trying to find out."[3]

THE MEDIA WE DEPEND ON

Media is often classified into four general types: print, broadcast, out-of-home, and internet. Print media includes newspapers, magazines, books, and direct mail, such as flyers and postcards. It is the oldest form of media. Broadcast media, or mass media, includes television, radio, and movies. Because it doesn't rely on reading, it reaches a larger audience than print media, including the illiterate. Out-of-home or outdoor media, such as billboards and signs, is used for advertising products and ideas. The newest form of media is the internet, or digital media. It is interactive and enables users to more easily choose the news they want. It includes email, social media, podcasts, online forums, and blogs. However, classifying media in this way can be too simplistic. Many news outlets present the same information in several forms. The *New York Times*, for example, publishes a daily print newspaper, has a website that publishes the same news online, and has a flourishing Twitter account. Many other news organizations do the same.

Digital technology enables vast amounts of data to be collected and spread. For example, cell phones were used to track the spread of COVID-19 in its early months. Print, broadcast, and digital media have all become major sources of information on COVID-19. Most people get news from more than one of these sources.

> ## VISUALIZING THE PANDEMIC
>
> Millions of people died during the COVID-19 pandemic. Words can be inadequate to express this enormous human toll. Graphs and numbers showing rising death tolls and lost jobs are impersonal and quickly become almost meaningless. Using telephoto lenses for safety, photographers made the COVID-19 tragedy real with visual messages showing the devastation behind the numbers: elderly patients on ventilators with loved ones viewing them through glass, medical staff wearing hazmat suits, and deserted city streets. Photographs captured the emotions triggered by the pandemic, from fear, grief, and loneliness to hope and determination.

People also distinguish between traditional or mainstream media and social media. Traditional or mainstream media pushes information in a single direction—from a provider to a customer. The sender decides what is published. Social media is electronic and two-way. Social media users can create and share their own content, messages, and information. Because it enables two-way communication, social media gives users much more freedom. Studies show that people consider mainstream media more credible than social media, even though they get most of their news from social media.

EARLY INFORMATION

Early in the pandemic, misinformation about COVID-19 began to spread throughout the media. One important factor driving this spread was social media. A responsible traditional news source tries to transmit factual information. It checks facts and validates the reliability of witnesses and sources before publishing. But social media platforms are designed to maximize user engagement, not the accuracy of their information. This can lead to promotion of political partisanship and distrust of authority.

Misinformation and disinformation both played a role in the pandemic. Misinformation is false or incorrect information presented with no motive. Early misinformation on the virus was due to incomplete or incorrect information. But very quickly, disinformation began to proliferate. Disinformation involves falsehoods or conspiracy theories and is deliberately spread for political or economic gain. Russia and China ran campaigns

Network television news is an example of mainstream media.

suggesting that health-care systems in democratic countries were failing and that only their authoritarian states could keep people safe. Other disinformation involved moneymaking scams promoting fake and potentially dangerous cures. Still other sources included racist and hate groups blaming Jews or immigrants for the virus or describing it as a secret government plot to control population growth.

By April 2020, almost 90 percent of Americans were closely following coronavirus news. In a study by the

> "Anything you say in advance of a pandemic seems alarmist. Anything that you've done after it starts is inadequate."[4]
>
> —Mike Leavitt, head of the Department of Health and Human Services from 2005 to 2009

23

COVID-19 BY THE NUMBERS

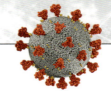

THE FIRST 14 WEEKS[5]

According to Project Information Literacy, three waves of media coverage occurred during the first 100 days of the COVID-19 pandemic, as shown by 125,696 online news stories published by 66 US news outlets between January 1 and April 9, 2020. News coverage started slowly when stories about an unknown but highly contagious virus began to emerge from China. The second wave tracked the spread of the virus around the world and monitored its expansion in the United States. The third wave occurred as case numbers and deaths rose to global pandemic levels.

Certain days in the three waves had spikes that led to a flurry of news stories. A January 15 spike during the first wave covered the first confirmed cases of COVID-19 in Thailand and Japan. During the second wave, articles on February 28 discussed Iran becoming a world COVID-19 hotspot, and articles from March 6 covered US college campuses as they began to close. During the third wave, peaks occurred when Trump declared a national emergency, the virus was ravaging New York City, Trump signed a stimulus bill to provide economic relief, and US jobless numbers rose to ten million.

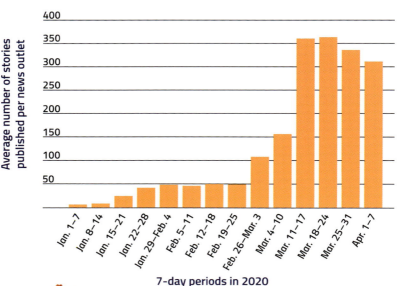

Pew Research Center, 70 percent said the news made them feel emotionally stressed, and many needed to take breaks from it. Half said they found it difficult to determine from the news what was true about the pandemic, and two-thirds reported seeing some stories that seemed completely made up.[6] As the pandemic heated up, many people were forced to shelter at home, cut off from personal contact. They became more and more invested in following the news.

MISINFORMATION AND DISINFORMATION

An example of misinformation was the CDC's early statement that masks were not effective against COVID-19. As more evidence became available, it reversed this statement. Disinformation is deliberately sharing incorrect information. One disinformation campaign claimed that Bill Gates, cofounder of Microsoft, planned to use a coronavirus vaccine to monitor people by injecting them with a microchip containing spy software. Another was a 26-minute video called *Plandemic*, released in May 2020, which—among other falsehoods—claimed that the COVID-19 virus was planted by global leaders to control the human population, that vaccines were harmful, and that wearing masks activated the virus. *Plandemic* was widely shared on Twitter and other social media platforms.

CHAPTER THREE

THE MAINSTREAM MEDIA

The mainstream media consists primarily of newspapers, magazines, television, and radio. Mainstream reporting on the COVID-19 pandemic has profoundly affected the general public. It has provided continuous information on the virus and its spread. It has provided information and advertisements on how to stay safe. It's helped keep the public updated on the latest statistics regarding numbers of cases and deaths from the virus. However, some segments of this media have also spread misinformation about the virus.

DECLINING TRUST IN THE MAINSTREAM MEDIA

A 2020 Gallup poll found that 60 percent of Americans have little or no trust in the media. Only 40 percent said

At the beginning of the pandemic, reporters presented stories about COVID-19 circulating through long-term care facilities.

they had either a great deal or a fair amount of trust. According to Gallup, the public's overall trust in mass media has declined considerably since the 1970s, when it ranged between 68 and 72 percent. In the 2020 poll, there was a huge gap in trust based on political party: 73 percent of Democrats but only 10 percent of Republicans expressed trust in media.[1] The Trust Barometer, an annual survey conducted by the communication firm Edelman, provides data on people's attitudes toward various institutions. In 2021, it found that fewer than half of all Americans trusted the mainstream media.[2] Survey respondents believed the media purposely tries to mislead people by making false or exaggerated

THE INFODEMIC

The Pan American Health Organization defines the term *infodemic* as "an over-abundance of information—some accurate and some not—that makes it hard for people to find trustworthy sources and reliable guidance."[3] The public needs clear, accurate information to make reasonable health decisions. When much of the information it receives is inaccurate, inconsistent, or conflicting, public health outcomes can suffer. People become confused about what steps to take. They may lose trust in those providing or reporting health recommendations and respond by refusing to carry out preventive measures that would protect their health and that of the general public.

statements and that it supports an ideology or political position instead of informing the public.

However, the media is not one thing, and people's level of trust varies. The media is diverse and complex. People might trust one media source and distrust another. Even a generally trustworthy source might have employees or subsidiaries that are more or less credible than the news organization generally is. Or people might trust the media's take on one topic but not another.

And trusting a source—that is, being convinced that its reporting is accurate and truthful—is not the same as agreeing with it. Many media consumers are less concerned with

> **TRUTH AND THE MAINSTREAM MEDIA**
>
> A study from Singapore highlighted the importance of the mainstream media in correcting misinformation early in the COVID-19 crisis. In the 164 articles examined, 59 percent of misinformation claims were totally fabricated; the rest contained a mix of true and false information. At first, misinformation related mostly to health and science issues. Later, issues of government policy and control measures dominated. As the mainstream media worked persistently to correct misinformation, the public's trust in Singapore's media increased to 50 percent in 2021, up from 42 percent during the same period in the previous year, before the COVID-19 pandemic hit the city.[4] These findings are consistent with those from countries around the world.

COVID-19 BY THE NUMBERS

HOW AMERICANS VIEW COVID-19 MEDIA COVERAGE[5]

The Pew Research Center conducted an online survey of Americans' attitudes toward the media's coverage of COVID-19 between April 20 and 26, 2020. The panel included 10,139 people from across the country. These pie charts compare attitudes of the survey group by political party—Democrats and Republicans. Some people failed to respond to the questions.

When looking at the response as a whole, a majority of people felt that the information was accurate and that the media was working to benefit the public. Smaller percentages took the opposite view. However, when broken out by political party, there was a sharp division between Republicans and Democrats. Democrats had a highly positive view of the media; Republicans had a more negative view.

NEWS ACCURACY BY POLITICAL PARTY

- News is largely accurate
- News is largely inaccurate
- Other

NEWS BENEFITS BY POLITICAL PARTY

- News is working for the public's benefit
- News is working for its own benefit
- Other

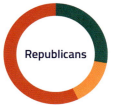

the truth and more insistent that the media take a partisan stance that agrees with their own. They distrust any media source that disagrees with them. At the same time, to keep ratings up, the mainstream media itself is becoming more ideology based. There is less neutral, fact-based reporting and more critiquing of opposing media. There is also a greater tendency toward sensationalism, with stories being written specifically to provoke strong emotions such as outrage.

COVID-19'S EFFECT ON TRUST IN MEDIA

The COVID-19 pandemic has affected media—and vice versa. As the pandemic accelerated, many people largely stayed home. They were afraid, and they needed information. Dependence on the media increased to all-time highs, but at the same time, distrust of it grew. The media has become increasingly polarized since the 1990s. Increased competition led media organizations to target specific demographics, such as people with particular political ideologies. Loss of jobs in local news media meant more reporting became concentrated in large cities, and people in smaller cities and rural communities began to feel journalists were out of touch

Many people questioned the reliability of the media during the pandemic.

with them. The pandemic further increased polarization. An August 2020 study at the University of Michigan concluded that newspaper stories and network news were highly politicized. One key pandemic issue that became polarized was mask mandates. At first, people debated whether wearing masks would slow or prevent transmission of the virus. There was little scientific data available about this issue early on. As the pandemic progressed, more studies showed the effectiveness of masks, but some people continued to doubt their usefulness. Some protested against mask mandates, saying that forcing them to wear masks was limiting their freedom.

But despite the polarization of media and the public's declining trust, people used mainstream media during the year of 2020 in greatly increased numbers. Television news had its highest audience numbers in years. In several European countries, including Norway, Finland, and Germany, commercial and public service news sites showed increases in weekly use by 9, 7, and 4 percentage points respectively, compared with pre-pandemic numbers.[6] Consumers particularly sought out fact-based, specialized coverage, including daily coronavirus data and explanatory information. Surveys done in January 2020 and a year later indicated that people turned to fact-based media more often during the pandemic, and trust in the mainstream media grew. According to the Digital News Report from Reuters Institute at Oxford University, United Kingdom, "Trust in the news (44 percent) is up six percentage points on average and considerably

> "I think that as journalists, we were disoriented at the beginning, and we probably didn't ask quite as many tough questions, like, 'Why wouldn't masks work?'"[7]
>
> —New York Times *health reporter Apoorva Mandavilli*

more than that in some countries." But this increase did not make up for the larger decline in trust over the past years. Also, 58 percent of respondents in a global sample said they had seen false or misleading information on COVID-19 in the week before the survey.[8] These numbers were higher in Africa and Latin America.

LOCAL AND REGIONAL MEDIA

One part of the mainstream media has been helped by the pandemic. Over the past few decades, local and regional media, such as newspapers, have been cutting staff as their audiences moved to free online news sources. But when COVID-19 hit, this changed. Sources in the United Kingdom reported that much of the news people needed was available only locally. Local news could tell people which hospitals were open, where COVID-19 testing sites were located, and what the local lockdown restrictions were. People quickly came to depend on their local sources again. Many local newspapers even went from weekly to daily publication schedules. People wanted facts immediately.

Besides facts, the local and regional papers provided another much-needed form of journalism:

good-news stories. Magazine editor Tracey Bagshaw from the United Kingdom said, "There were lots of pictures of people painting rainbows and delivering food and, you know, just helping others."[9]

These positive stories attracted large numbers of readers. During the pandemic, local media also provided print subscriptions as gifts and tried out new technologies and software to simplify interviewing people from home and keeping reporters connected. In short, the media used journalism skills to ease readers' and employees' emotional stress as well as provide information.

There was no guarantee that this expanded role of local and regional media would continue after the

---

LESSENING EMOTIONAL TRAUMA

In stressful situations such as the COVID-19 pandemic, when people were fearful and rarely left their homes, many dealt with anxiety or depression. The media can help alleviate stress levels and increase people's emotional stability by keeping them connected, entertained, and informed. During the pandemic, the media was vital in maintaining its users' emotional health. Platforms such as Facebook and Instagram posted many videos on emotional health and advertised others. Publishers such as Scholastic provided free books for young children; they and others created online activities for kids of all ages. Toy companies ran huge discounts on educational toys, which the media advertised.

HOW HEALTH ORGANIZATIONS USE MEDIA

Health organizations are a major source of information about COVID-19. To effectively communicate this information, they must use media well. They must frame their message carefully, present up-to-date information, and communicate honestly what is known and not known about the pandemic and the virus. Also, the weight given to particular issues can completely change the way the public understands the information. Issues that might be emphasized or ignored in providing health information include health, preparedness, social welfare, governance and institutions, politics, and the economy.

pandemic, but one person expected it would. Alastair Machray, former editor-in-chief of the *Liverpool Echo*, said, "My sense is that the reputation of the regional media has been enhanced massively through COVID due to the efforts and expertise they've expended on behalf of their readership."[10]

ROLE OF MEDIA IN PROMOTING SAFETY

One final and vital role of media during the COVID-19 pandemic was promoting safety. Often, these safety messages came from medical or public health organizations and were transmitted by both the mainstream media and social media. The American Public Health Association, for example, used a short and simple phrase to highlight the three most important safety precautions: Wash your hands, wear a mask, and keep your distance. It tried to make sure the public received the message through news shows, public service messages, and commercials. Other organizations that promoted the same precautions, often with explanations of how and why they were important, included the WHO, the CDC, and health departments of important universities including Harvard.

In the COVID-19 era, everyone—including the mainstream media—made mistakes, because the world was dealing with a new, unknown menace. But the mainstream media was and remains a vital source of information for people around the world.

The media helped raise awareness of the importance of wearing masks and washing or sanitizing hands frequently to stay healthy.

CHAPTER FOUR

SOCIAL MEDIA

Social media has grown by leaps and bounds over the past couple of decades. It is the primary source of news for many people and one of several news sources for many others. Social media has influenced the spreading of good news and useful information about COVID-19, as well as the spreading of misinformation. Certain types of news have dominated the scene. Most data suggests that social media can have either helpful or harmful impacts on people's physical and social well-being, depending on who is posting.

POSITIVE IMPACTS OF SOCIAL MEDIA

One important way in which people have used social media during the pandemic is to obtain health information. In a study done in Bangladesh, two-thirds of those questioned used social media for this purpose. Most of the users were college students. They obtained

During the pandemic, social media allowed people to stay connected through their devices. But there were some unhelpful things about it too.

SOCIAL MEDIA, POSITIVE AND NEGATIVE

A study of 18- to 24-year-olds in the Asia Pacific region (Australia, China, Hong Kong, and Singapore) suggested that social media was a double-edged sword during the pandemic. About one-fourth of the young people in the study said that being able to interact with friends and family through social media helped their mood and well-being. Social media had also provided a distraction, helped combat boredom, and provided a source of news. But more than one-third of the people in the study said that social media had decreased their well-being, mostly because the large number of negative stories had increased their stress.[2]

most of their health information from television and from social media, particularly Facebook. About 87 percent of social media users in the study followed suggested health guidelines. They were three times more likely to follow these guidelines than nonusers and were especially likely to follow social distancing guidelines.[1] This study suggested that social media had a positive impact on the handling of the COVID-19 pandemic in Bangladesh.

A study at the University of California, Berkeley, showed a positive effect of social media use on mental health as well. The study was done on students at 65 high schools in Peru during the pandemic. Adolescents in the study who developed peer relationships online during the lockdown were less lonely than those who did not, said study director Lucía Magis-Weinberg. The study suggested that parents of adolescents should promote rather than limit screen time and that the amount of time spent online is less important than its quality.

Among the mental health consequences of a long-term lockdown and social isolation are increased stress, anxiety, depression, eating disorders, and post-traumatic stress disorder. The increased loneliness resulting from lockdown leads to a decline in happiness. These mental health symptoms have been documented in China, the United States, and Israel.

In Belgium from March 18 through May 4, 2020, almost all businesses and organizations were closed. Face-to-face interactions were restricted to those

SOCIAL MEDIA AND HEALTH INFORMATION

Social media became a popular source of health information about COVID-19, offering platforms where individuals can access medical information, data, and opinions. Government agencies, such as the CDC and the National Institutes of Health, provided frequently updated reports on the virus, disease, symptoms, and vaccines on platforms such as Facebook. Experts on infectious diseases, such as National Institute of Allergy and Infectious Diseases director Anthony Fauci, often appeared in videos with YouTube stars to help educate younger people.

in the same household. A study on the mental health consequences of COVID-19 was done on Belgian adolescents. Three forms of social media coping were studied: active coping, social relation coping, and humorous coping. In active coping, people carry out specific actions designed to reduce their anxiety. For example, they might seek out information or actively change their behavior. In social relation coping, they might relieve fear or depression by interacting with friends

Social media helped adolescents stay connected even when they were isolated at home.

and family on social media. In humorous coping, they might entertain themselves by seeking out humorous videos or playing games. This relieves stress by taking their minds off the pandemic.

Most adolescents in the study used social media to regulate their moods. Overall, using social media relieved stress and anxiety. But it did not make up for the loss of personal contact. While using social media was helpful in some ways, it did not increase happiness.

Social media can play a positive role in buffering the effects of a pandemic and making people more resilient in coping with the danger. It provides a way for people to send facts and relay opinions about the crisis and to voice their fears. The threats of COVID-19 changed with time, making it difficult for people to adapt. The massive amount of information out there, some correct and some false, further complicated the situation.

NEGATIVE IMPACTS OF SOCIAL MEDIA

Misinformation about COVID-19 is widespread and hard to combat. It includes false and sometimes dangerous ideas. For example, some people promoted the idea that COVID-19 could be cured by ingesting methanol or other toxic substances. Professor Norbert Schwarz, a psychologist at the University of Southern California, lists five criteria used to determine if information is true: compatibility with known information, credibility of the source, whether others believe it, whether it is internally consistent, and whether there is evidence for it. But information is also more likely to be accepted if it is easy to understand. And an overriding factor is whether the information fits the person's own biases. If so, the person is more likely to accept the information, whether or not it is true.

Under certain circumstances, social media can

BELIEVING MISINFORMATION

Filippo Menczer, professor of informatics and computer science, and Thomas Hills, professor of psychology, described in a 2020 article how people come to believe misinformation. They illustrated this with an invented person they call Andy. At first, Andy is afraid of contracting COVID-19. He gets tips and information from friends and colleagues. Someone on Facebook says COVID-19 fears are overblown. Then the hotel where Andy works closes, and he fears for his job. He begins to think the COVID-19 story might be overblown. A colleague posts an article blaming pharmaceutical companies and politicians for creating a COVID-19 scare. He's never trusted the government. Then Andy reads a false article saying that COVID-19 is no worse than the flu. He is now a believer that the COVID-19 pandemic is a hoax.

negatively affect mental and emotional health. In one study, exposure to as little as two minutes of negative COVID-related news on Twitter or YouTube decreased emotional well-being. However, many people spend much more time consuming pandemic news. Almost half of the people in the study spent at least 30 minutes per day consuming pandemic news, causing the researchers to state, "The present findings likely offer a conservative estimate of the emotional toll of interacting with COVID-related media in the real world."[3] The response to positive COVID-19 news, such as uplifting stories describing acts of kindness, does not result in negative feelings; in fact, the response is often positive. Thus, the problem is likely not the amount of time on social media but the intake of negative information.

 Researchers are studying the flow of information on social media, including the method by and speed with which it spreads. There are several reasons why it is difficult to control the spread of misinformation. First, when a person hears and accepts a piece of misinformation, that person will often continue to believe it even after the statement is corrected and the reasons for the misstatement are explained. This person maintains the belief because of biases. For example, according to Peter Ditto of the University of California, Irvine, people tend to use skepticism selectively, tending not to criticize statements that align with their political beliefs.

Second, many people do not really evaluate the information. They simply read it and pass it on. They are passive sharers, rather than malicious spreaders of misinformation. If people's thinking and reasoning is based more on intuition or gut feelings than on careful

Misinformation can be spread on a variety of social media platforms. It is important to use discernment when reading information on these apps.

reasoning, they are more likely to be drawn in and believe false information. Other research shows that people holding extreme political beliefs are also very susceptible to misinformation. Older adults tend to share more information—both true and fake—about COVID-19, but younger people tend to be more likely to believe misinformation. Researchers are working to understand the types of people who spread and believe fake news. They know it cannot be stopped, but their goal is to slow its spread.

HOW TO SPOT COVID-19 MISINFORMATION

Benjamin Bell and Fergal Gallagher of ABC News say that the best way to spot misinformation about COVID-19 is to consider the source. Bell and Gallagher recommend that if people don't recognize the source of the information they are reading, they should look it up. They list several sources that should not be trusted. First are conspiracy theorists. These people often develop complex, hard-to-follow theories to explain situations. Their theories may blame corporations, wealthy individuals, or other groups for masterminding disasters such as the

WHICH MEDIA DO PEOPLE BELIEVE?

People who get their news from social media are more likely to believe misinformation about COVID-19, including conspiracies and incorrect information about risk factors and preventive measures. Those who obtain their news from local television networks, community newspapers, news websites, or apps are considerably less likely to believe inaccurate claims. Of 21,000 US citizens surveyed between August 7 and August 26, 2020, those believing inaccurate claims included 28 percent of Snapchat users and 23 percent of Instagram users. Of those who received news from local television news, news websites, or community newspapers, just 11 percent believed inaccurate claims.[4] This data appears to confirm fears that social media contributes to misinformation about COVID-19.

COVID-19 pandemic. The second untrustworthy group is scammers. These people tend to prey on scared, vulnerable consumers, urging them to spend money on fake cures and other bogus products.

Politicians, both in the United States and around the world, have also spread misinformation and disinformation on COVID-19. In either case, it should be checked—such people are not medical experts. Neither are celebrities or most family members and friends, who often weigh in on topics such as COVID-19. One group that has spread misinformation is anti-vaxxers, a term for people who oppose vaccines. These people generally believe that vaccines are dangerous and should be avoided based on a now discredited study that linked vaccine use with autism.[5] The anti-vax position gained more traction with the COVID-19 pandemic as supporters urged people not to take COVID-19 vaccines. A final group to know about is satirists. These people publish work that is satire, humorous, and often exaggerated or invented to entertain readers, make a point, or both. Such publications are generally labeled as satire, but occasionally people take their words as truth. A good example is the online satirical newspaper *The Onion*.

> "The fundamental problem with misinformation is that once people have heard it, they tend to believe and act on it, even after it's been corrected."[6]
>
> —*Stephan Lewandowsky, professor of psychology, University of Bristol, United Kingdom*

Social media is an important source of news and information on COVID-19. Because of its free, unfiltered nature, the news it spreads can be true or untrue, and it is up to the receiver of that information to decide what to believe.

CHAPTER FIVE

HOW MEDIA USE CHANGED

COVID-19 has had a profound effect on how people use media, particularly online media, and how often they use it. During the months of lockdowns, when most schools and businesses were closed, people used the internet to work and attend school. They began to do more shopping online, and they talked to friends and relatives via video calls rather than in person. There has also been a shift in the types of content posted on social media. Some, but not all, of these trends may become permanent.

CHANGING NUMBERS

According to the media measurement firm eMarketer, Americans in 2020 spent an average of 82 minutes per day on social media—up seven minutes from 2019.[1]

Teachers and students had to adjust to holding classes online during parts of the pandemic.

SOCIAL MEDIA AND MENTAL HEALTH

In August 2020, during the COVID-19 pandemic, the CDC published a report showing a decline in US mental health. Thirty-one percent of those studied reported feeling anxiety or depression, 26 percent showed stress-related symptoms, 13 percent had started or increased drug use, and 11 percent had suicidal thoughts.[4] In China, questionnaires given to college students between March 24 and April 1, 2020, showed a link between higher use of social media and depression. Another global study cited increasing evidence that constant news reports of rising COVID-19 cases and death rates negatively affects people's mental health.

Another major study of internet users through September 2020 found that social media consumption increased by 72 percent and posting by 43 percent. Instagram users increased their usage by 69 percent during lockdown. Most users remained with platforms they had already been using. Of those trying a new platform, 33 percent chose TikTok. This is one of the three platforms most used for escape or entertainment; the other two were Instagram and YouTube. Most people did not avoid any of their usual social media platforms, but of those who did, 20 percent avoided Facebook, and 12 percent avoided Twitter.[2]

A Harris poll conducted from late March to early May 2020 showed that between 46 and 51 percent of people were using social media more than before the pandemic.[3]

The poll report stressed that this usage might change again, decreasing as people returned to work and school. However, the researchers expected several trends to continue, resulting in a permanent shift in internet usage. One of these was the use of Zoom and other platforms for business conferencing, replacing some business travel. They expected mobile messaging and use of services such as Facebook Messenger, WhatsApp, and Apple iMessage to remain higher. Platforms such as Instagram and Snapchat—and to a lesser extent, Facebook—were also expected to sustain their boost in usage after the pandemic.

CHANGING CONTENT

In September 2020, the organization Digital Commerce 360 surveyed more than 4,500 Influenster

> ### IS MY POSTING INAPPROPRIATE?
>
> It may seem natural for people to post to social media more often during a pandemic. It is a way to connect to friends and loved ones when personal visits are not possible. But what should people post? To one user, named Mona, posting her usual fare—about her workouts and getting in shape, for example—seemed in poor taste, considering that so many people were dying in the outside world. "It feels so silly to show happy stories in a pandemic," she said in an interview with Vox. "Everything feels inappropriate."[5]

CONFIRMATION BIAS

One negative aspect of social media use may be an increase in social anxiety. People using social media to feel more connected may see how disconnected they really are. When they compare their own lives with exaggerated online descriptions of positive experiences, they may give in to confirmation bias—that is, their already negative opinions of themselves intensify. According to Jeremy Tyler, a psychiatrist at the Perelman School of Medicine, "People see other users who appear to be perfect, who are well liked, or who have things they may not, and they start to believe some of the negative perceptions about themselves."[7]

community members in North America. Many users of this site, which sends users products or services to review on social media, saw a major change in the types of content posted on various platforms. While 42 percent said the content they posted did not change, 33 percent said their feeds had changed from selfies, life updates, and generally positive posts to content that was "overwhelming," "stressful," or marked by "information overload."[6] Most also said that content was much more political than before the pandemic.

While enabling connection with friends and family, social media services such as Twitter also became a source of real-time news about the pandemic. The shared experience of the pandemic brought media users together and gave them a feeling of usefulness.

Jordan Updike of Indianapolis, Indiana, got COVID-19 early in the pandemic and was still suffering side effects a year later. During this time, concerned that many people were not taking the pandemic seriously, he began discussing it on social media. "I realized even if I have conversations with one person, there were hundreds if not thousands of people observing that conversation," Updike said. "If it meant 20 people changing their minds or taking this thing seriously, I felt that that was time well spent."[8]

> "We shouldn't use social media to reproduce pre-pandemic normality, we should be using it to create a new normal."[9]
> —Thomas Roach, professor of cultural studies, Bryant University

EVERYDAY LIFE GOES ONLINE

For many people, work, school, shopping, and entertainment became online activities during the pandemic. But according to the Digital Commerce 360 poll, while online work, school, and entertainment may have been new to many users, online shopping was not. More than half of users said they shopped online before the pandemic and continued to do so.

For more than a year, work and school were entirely online for many people. Work meetings occurred on Zoom, Google Hangouts, and Microsoft Teams. School assignments were made via Google Classroom. While some teachers posted about exciting online activities they were conducting with their students, others found online schooling stressful. They had difficulties ensuring that their students had broadband access and could get their online lessons. They had concerns about their students' mental health, as the students suffered from fatigue, isolation, and being surrounded by fear, illness, and sometimes death.

Entertainment outside the home became more and more difficult as COVID-19 cases rose. Instead, people

It was harder for teachers to assess how their students were doing emotionally when classes were held online.

turned to online services such as Netflix and YouTube. With college and professional sports seasons canceled, people turned instead to video games. The leading site for streaming video games, Twitch, showed a 20 percent surge in user traffic by the end of March 2020.[10] The use of TikTok, which shows short video clips, was already rising before the pandemic and continued to rise during it.

CONTROLLING INFORMATION

The types of information published on social media has been extremely helpful to the public. For example, health information can increase public health awareness and initiate behavioral changes. But social media companies cannot easily limit the spread of

ONLINE DATING

Given lockdowns to prevent catching a deadly disease, one might have expected dating to decline during COVID-19. Instead, online dating surged, with video chats replacing face-to-face interactions. In March 2020, Tinder recorded three billion swipes in one day. Between March and May, dates rose on dating sites. OKCupid dates increased by 700 percent and Bumble video calls by 70 percent. In the real world, dates continued too—but with precautions.[11] A typical date was outdoors and involved social distancing and masks. Both parties had to agree when to move indoors and remove masks. As vaccinations became available, the rules relaxed, but some daters remained cautious.

US surgeon general Vivek Murthy spoke about the dangers of misinformation on various platforms, including on social media, on July 15, 2021.

malicious and untrue material, even if they want to. Online extremists use emotional responses to posts to fuel their conspiracy theories and lure in new followers. But the information is not confined to a single media platform. Although each platform has its own rules, platforms are connected through their user communities—for example, many Facebook users are also on Twitter and Instagram. Thus, these users spread information—true and untrue— across multiple platforms. Some platforms are not as well moderated as others. They may not remove posts after a certain time period or link posts to specific user accounts. These differences make it more difficult to moderate overall media content.

Links between these decentralized platforms can quickly spread content from one to another. Suppose a piece of misinformation appears on Facebook, and Facebook detects and removes it. But before it is removed, that piece of misinformation has already been shared on Twitter and spreads there. Then, people on Twitter send it back to Facebook. No single platform can control the spread of information, true or untrue. Even if all media companies agreed to cooperate, extremist content would still appear. Alternative platforms and media networks exist that bypass standard social media platforms to spread this content. Instead of trying to help control malicious content, these platforms look for new and better ways to share and spread it. Researchers, including some at George Washington University, are working to find ways to help reduce the spread of misinformation and disinformation on social media.

> "We see so much misinformation because the platforms have no real interest in deterring it. . . . Actually, the platforms profit from it because the more outrageous the content the more people interact with it."[12]
>
> —Roger Entner, technology and telecommunications analyst, Recon Analytics

CHAPTER SIX

THE INTRODUCTION OF COVID-19 VACCINES

The development of a vaccine for COVID-19 was a breakthrough in controlling the pandemic. After months of media coverage of rising case numbers, rising death rates, and shortages of equipment, supplies, and medical personnel, there was finally good news. The disease could not be cured, but with a vaccine, the virus that causes COVID-19 could be prevented from taking hold in a person's body.

In the United States, the biotechnology company Moderna began clinical trials in mid-March 2020. Vaccine development received a huge boost in May with the launch of the Trump administration's Operation Warp Speed, which provided $10 billion to support companies developing vaccines.[1] By cutting out the waiting time built into the usual drug-approval process

President Donald Trump's administration began Operation Warp Speed to help accelerate the development of a COVID-19 vaccine.

GETTING RELIABLE COVID-19 INFORMATION

Much of the COVID-19 information reaching the public through traditional news media came from government sources such as the Food and Drug Administration (FDA) and CDC or from independent medical and research groups such as the American Medical Association, Mayo Clinic, Kaiser Family Foundation, and Johns Hopkins Medicine. These sources provided information in short, easy-to-understand segments. They included facts about how the vaccines were being developed and tested. They also discussed vaccine safety and explained possible risks.

without skipping the research or safety tests, scientists decreased the development time for the first COVID-19 vaccines by an average of 3.9 years. The first vaccines were authorized for emergency use in December 2020—the Pfizer vaccine on December 11 and the Moderna on December 18. The first vaccines were given in New York City on December 14, 2020. According to the CDC, only 11 months elapsed from development to authorization of emergency use for the vaccines.[2]

The public desperately wanted a way to control the impact of the COVID-19 pandemic. But at the same time, many people worried about the safety of the vaccines because of their rapid development. Some wondered whether scientists were cutting corners or skipping some of the usual testing phases. Journalists wrote articles explaining that all the normal phases were completed and the vaccines were safe. Vaccines typically go through three trial phases, one after another. For the COVID-19 vaccines, the urgent situation led scientists to overlap the three phases to accelerate the process. Also, COVID-19 is a coronavirus, similar to the viruses that cause flu, colds, and two previously known diseases, SARS and MERS. Scientists were familiar with these diseases and the viruses that cause them. They had already researched vaccines against these diseases, so they were not starting from scratch against COVID-19. But for the public to accept the

Media outlets covered the vaccinations of prominent people in the government, including that of Illinois attorney general Kwame Raoul.

vaccines, they had to be reassured about how the vaccines were made and tested.

VACCINE DEVELOPMENT

Getting a vaccine from the research laboratory into the bodies of the public requires communication. People must know about the vaccine, it must be available to them, and they must be willing to take it. The media helps people understand the science of vaccines and how they will affect health. It can greatly influence how the public perceives vaccine risk and how likely people are to carry out protective behaviors, including taking vaccines.

> "The most important ingredient in all vaccines is trust."[3]
> —Barry Bloom, Harvard T. H. Chan School of Public Health

A study from a Brazilian university compared media coverage at large newspapers in the United States, the United Kingdom, and Brazil. Researchers compared media coverage of vaccines in the three countries. They analyzed articles on vaccines from one major newspaper in each country (the *New York Times*, the *Guardian*, and *Folha de São Paolo*) published between January 1 and

October 31, 2020. These three newspapers are generally considered to be trustworthy.

The study's authors emphasized the media's responsibility to provide the public with accurate, unbiased information and noted that several aspects of media coverage on the COVID-19 pandemic could be considered biased. Often, the newspapers described research toward a COVID-19 vaccine as a race or competition between countries. Vaccines were described not by their laboratory of origin but by country. Researchers wrote that characterizing the search in this way could produce bias, especially since article titles are brief, incomplete, and designed to capture the reader's attention rather than to educate or inform. A further concern was the tendency to focus articles on

VACCINE MYTHS

The CDC cautions people to be sure their COVID-19 information, including vaccine information, is accurate and comes from a credible source. It compiled a list of some common myths based on misinformation from noncredible sources. One myth says that COVID-19 vaccines contain microchips designed to track your movements. Another states that receiving a COVID-19 vaccine causes people to be magnetic. Other myths warn that COVID-19 vaccines change DNA and that getting a COVID-19 vaccine gives people COVID-19.

politics rather than science. This tendency was more pronounced in the Brazilian and American newspapers. Researchers feared that such politicization of science prevented adoption of science-based actions that would benefit people's lives, such as getting vaccinated. They also stated that the newspapers failed to focus on other important issues, such as the actions of the WHO and social justice in accessing vaccines.

VACCINE HESITANCY

Once vaccines were available, one might think the pandemic problem would be solved. While the virus would not magically disappear, most of the population would soon be vaccinated and—like measles, polio, or the flu—COVID-19 would be present in the population but as a lesser threat. However, this optimistic outlook failed to consider vaccine hesitancy, which means people hesitate or refuse to take vaccines. Some of this hesitancy can be traced to safety fears based on the speed of vaccine development and some to mistrust in the government dispensing the vaccines. In other cases, people were not hesitant to get vaccinated, but for various reasons, such as a lack of transportation, childcare, or time off from work;

Some people held protests against vaccine mandates. They expressed their mistrust in the vaccines and government agencies.

disabilities; or language barriers, they were unable to get vaccinated.

Since the first vaccine, for smallpox in 1798, people have spoken out against vaccines, sometimes using misinformation or disinformation to spread their message. Also, there were several instances early in vaccine development when severe side effects occurred. This happened with the polio virus in 1955. A batch of vaccine was released in which the polio virus was supposed to be inactivated but was not. Two hundred children were paralyzed and ten died. Although vaccine development now is much safer and more precise, some people still fear vaccines. All of this has led to vaccine hesitancy.

VACCINATION AND GOVERNMENTS

Getting a large portion of the public to take a vaccine in part requires trust in the vaccine, which is closely tied to trust in the government delivering it. Around the world, public trust in governments is low, making it difficult to persuade people to get vaccinated. To increase people's trust in government, the Organisation for Economic Co-operation and Development (OECD) suggests several strategies for governments, including releasing timely information about vaccines, being transparent in public communications, and listening to and addressing people's concerns.

According to the WHO, this hesitancy is causing a global health threat. This is a signal for the media to step up and play its vital part: providing the public with correct information on vaccines, their use, and their safety. One group that plays a major role in informing the public is the public service media (PSM). The PSM includes broadcasting that is made, financed, and controlled by the public. It is intended to be nonpartisan, independent, and run for the benefit of the public. The PSM also has experience reporting on vaccine hesitancy.

The PSM's journalists often have greater access than most private broadcasters to isolated, low-income, and ethnic minority communities, enabling them to more easily provide accurate information on vaccines to more people. Also, the public wants information it can trust. Although trust in the media has declined in recent years, the PSM is among the most trusted media in many places around the world. This means people are more likely to believe information from this source and therefore less likely to be vaccine hesitant.

The Public Media Alliance stresses that the role of the PSM is to serve the public. Desilon Daniels of the Public Media Alliance noted that the PSM needs to provide the public with "information that is factual, balanced, and aids in the making of well-informed decisions."[4] This means overcoming COVID-19 vaccine misinformation. Ways it can do this include fact-checking, making sure information on vaccine development and impact is science-based, and reporting concerns about vaccines responsibly.

Of course, development and distribution of COVID-19 vaccines was essential. But once the vaccines became available, much of the responsibility for delivering a successful vaccination campaign fell on the media. Without media input of careful, accurate, nonbiased information about vaccines and their safety, vaccination numbers may remain low, leading to a greater spread of COVID-19 than initially hoped for.

CHAPTER SEVEN

MEDIA BIAS

As the COVID-19 pandemic progressed, fear and uncertainty were heightened by squabbles within the media and between the media and politicians. Early in the pandemic, people wanted information on the virus, but officials were not always transparent. Later, individuals and political parties disagreed about whether to wear masks, close public places, or otherwise act to slow the spread of the virus. After vaccines became available, media and political bias surged, and anti-vaxxers made the news.

One scandal involving control of information took place in New York. At first, many news sources highly praised Governor Andrew Cuomo for his handling of the pandemic. He gave frequent televised briefings highlighting the state's successes. However, some people were concerned about a directive that required nursing homes to take patients who were

Many news outlets at first praised New York governor Andrew Cuomo for his early efforts during the pandemic.

recovering from COVID-19. They worried that this would spread the disease and cause many unnecessary deaths. Later, as nursing-home deaths from COVID-19 rose, Cuomo was accused by state health department officials of underreporting these deaths. Cuomo said the accusations were politically motivated, but an investigation in early 2021 showed that there were several thousand more nursing-home deaths than reported. The *New York Times* shared those discrepancies. Cuomo later admitted to lowering the count, saying he feared the Trump administration would use the numbers as a political weapon.

Governor Cuomo resigned in August 2021 because of an unrelated scandal. In late August the new governor, Kathy Hochul, announced that New York's total number of COVID-19 deaths, not just those in nursing homes, had been underreported. On August 24, his last day in office, Cuomo had announced that the death toll was 43,400. On August 25, Governor Hochul raised the actual number to 55,400.[1] Until Cuomo's misreporting of COVID-19 deaths was uncovered, he had received strong praise from most major news outlets, including the *New York Times*, CNN, and MSNBC. He was praised for holding press conferences and appearing open to the public, while his policy actions were largely ignored. This episode led to a further distrust in the media. As Ross Barkan of *Columbia Journalism Review* asked, "Why weren't harder questions posed?"[2]

WEARING MASKS—YES OR NO?

Throughout the pandemic, there were extreme opinions on both sides of issues such as mask wearing. Social media platforms including Facebook, Twitter, Reddit, and YouTube brought these marginal groups to the attention of millions of people. Mainstream media helped push

Frequent coverage of protests sometimes made certain viewpoints seem more widely held than they actually were.

TOO MUCH MEDIA COVERAGE

During November 2020, several groups of people protesting masks made headlines around Canada. Researcher Aengus Bridgman pointed out that both mainstream and social media often exaggerate the numbers of people resisting masks by giving them disproportionate coverage. "It's really important to note that from 85 to 90 percent of Canadians are wearing masks regularly," Bridgman said.[3]

the visibility of mask resistance in attempts to cover both sides of the story. For example, Canadian PhD student Aengus Bridgman studied how people participate in politics online. He examined media reports on masking. He found that when health authorities counseled against wearing masks, media reports suggested masks could help prevent spread of the virus. But when governments decided masks were helpful, the media also changed course and questioned their effectiveness.

The media's influence on mask-wearing attitudes was also shown by a University of Oregon study of Twitter posts between March and August 2020. Of more than 149,000 Twitter posts, 93 percent were pro–mask wearing, with only 7 percent opposed. One of the researchers, linguist Zhuo Jing-Schmidt, said the polarization of tweets was extreme, with many being "angry and shouty."[4] But those resisting masks were a very small group. Jing-Schmidt said media coverage amplified the issue of resisting the use of masks. Polarizing hashtags were associated with story headlines focusing on anti-mask sentiment.

Observers sometimes criticized what they saw as hypocrisy by the media. For example, the tabloid the *New York Post* was critical of public health officials and guidance on wearing masks and getting vaccinated. Yet in the *Post*'s own newsroom, the newspaper required its employees to wear masks and follow other COVID-19 protocols recommended by health officials.

WEARING MASKS OUTDOORS

Some mask wearers responded harshly to those who didn't wear masks in low-risk situations, such as outdoor settings where people were social distancing. Especially for vaccinated people, scientists found that this setting posed little risk of infection. The CDC updated its guidelines to reflect the increasing safety of outdoor activities, and in the spring of 2021, at least one newspaper suggested an end to outdoor mask wearing. Although this article was approved by top public health experts, some people reacted angrily, saying it was "shallow and selfish" and implying that not wearing masks made non–mask wearers guilty of killing others.[5]

WHO ARE THE UNVACCINATED?

Vaccines for COVID-19 have been available since December 2020 and have been shown to save lives. But many people are still unvaccinated. They have a variety of reasons for being unvaccinated. Not all of them are strongly opposed to all vaccines.

Rhea Boyd is a pediatrician and public-health advocate in the San Francisco Bay Area. She codeveloped a campaign called The Conversation that works to provide correct information and dispel misinformation about vaccines. Her discussions with many diverse groups of people gave her insight into variations among unvaccinated people. She stated, "Unvaccinated people aren't a random group of defectors who are trying to be deviant. They're not all anti-vaxxers."[6]

Some unvaccinated people worry about side effects and wonder whether the vaccines are safe. Many people lack basic credible information about vaccines. They may not have access to the internet or may be reacting to disinformation embedded in their news sources. Also, just because vaccines are available does not mean everyone has access to them. If the nearest vaccination location is miles away, people may be unable to take advantage of it because they lack transportation or childcare or cannot take time off work. Such people include those in rural areas and those with low incomes.

Other people fear taking vaccines for different reasons. Some fear possible allergic reactions. Some give religious reasons. Some think vaccines cause the disease or lead to conditions such as autism. Other people mistrust pharmaceutical companies, worrying their main goal is to make money, not to protect people.

Much of the US anti-vaccine sentiment appeared to be generated by online promoters of vaccine disinformation. According to a March 2021 study by two groups, the Center for Countering Digital Hate (CCDH) and Anti-Vax Watch, just 12 individuals or organizations are responsible

> **DEATH OVER VACCINES?**
>
> Stephen Harmon, 34, mocked vaccinations on social media and refused the COVID-19 vaccination. He died in July 2021 following a monthlong battle with COVID-19. Shortly before he was hospitalized, he tweeted, "I got 99 problems but a vax ain't one." Oren Friedman, who treated COVID-19 patients at Cedar-Sinai Medical Center in Los Angeles, said Harmon's death was "unbelievably demoralizing." According to Friedman, "Virtually every single person that is getting sick enough to be admitted to the hospital has not been vaccinated."[7]

for 65 percent of the anti-vaccine content found on Facebook, Twitter, and Instagram. Imran Ahmed, the CEO of CCDH, said the efforts of this "Disinformation Dozen" represent "a targeted campaign to mislead Americans about the safety of the COVID-19 vaccines."[8] Their disinformation violated the terms of use agreements of all three social media platforms. CCDH and Anti-Vax Watch urged the social media sites to remove these people and groups from their platforms. However, these sites try to avoid censoring people who are simply expressing

Some people worked to counter misinformation and teach people about COVID-19 through theater.

concern. According to spokesperson Elizabeth Busby of Twitter, the platform seeks to distinguish between "harmful vaccine misinformation that contradicts credible public health information, which is prohibited under our policy, and negative vaccine sentiment that is a matter of opinion."9

Others do not think that removing even disinformation about the COVID-19 vaccines is helpful. According to Richard Armitage of the University of Nottingham's Division of Epidemiology and Public Health, censoring false information could silence those who have genuine concerns and are looking for clear answers because they feel worried about being shamed for having such concerns. He also said that making laws to allow the removal of disinformation "would enforce censorship and

A REFORMED ANTI-VAXXER

Craig Idlebrook became an anti-vaxxer because he wanted to live more naturally for his own health and that of the planet. He surrounded himself with friends and news sources who reinforced his opinions. He refused to get his daughter vaccinated. Idlebrook's journey back to science was slow, helped by people who urged him to reevaluate his beliefs and by a job that taught him about the FDA's drug approval process. His daughter and younger son received their vaccinations, and he was vaccinated for COVID-19. He now advocates online for COVID-19 vaccinations.

deplatforming and threaten the democratic cornerstone of freedom of speech. All ideas—even the bad ones—must be allowed a public airing, and their qualities debated in the marketplace of ideas. It is through this process that institutions foster influence, respect and public trust, by presenting empirical evidence, reasoned arguments and a scientific method based on critical thinking."[10] Armitage added that removing disinformation would only cause those who believe it to become even more convinced that there are conspiracies surrounding the vaccines.

VACCINES AND MEDIA BIAS

The vaccine controversy during the COVID-19 pandemic was marked by both political and media bias. Different media outlets took opposite sides on vaccines and frequently failed to present both sides of the issue. Media sites are becoming more politically partisan. Because individuals seek out sites that conform to their own beliefs, people often get their news from a closed echo chamber that reinforces their biases and prevents them from seeing the whole picture.

Social media bias is fed by the algorithms used by sites such as Facebook to ensure that users keep clicking. Algorithms are computer programs designed to give users what they want. If a user interacts with a Facebook post, Facebook's algorithm assumes the user is interested in that post and gives them more of the same. The more a statement is repeated, the more likely people are to believe it, whether it is true or not. Also, information that has an emotional impact, such as name-calling, resonates more strongly with people. And people tend to seek out facts that reinforce what they want to believe, regardless of whether it is true. Social media algorithms reinforce all these tendencies.

> "Social media . . . is designed to reinforce your beliefs, not challenge them."[11]
>
> —F. Perry Wilson, MD, MSCE, Yale School of Medicine

In short, media bias has operated throughout the COVID-19 pandemic. This is not surprising—the media is composed of individuals, all of whom have their own biases. Overcoming bias is a challenge that the media will continue to face into the future.

CHAPTER EIGHT

FROM PANDEMIC TO PART OF LIFE

With the distribution of vaccines in 2021 and the protection they provided, life appeared to return to a modified form of normal. Observers of the news media and the media itself began stepping back to consider how they had handled this crisis. They asked what the media had done right and wrong and how US coverage compared with coverage around the world.

When the pandemic hit, journalism was already under financial and political pressure, and it already was dealing with a flood of misinformation. The public clamored for correct, reliable information. The media had to deliver the words of doctors, scientists, and public health officials to the public while maintaining journalistic standards and making a profit. Budget cuts meant fewer science reporters, and sometimes

The media reported the statements of many health experts, including those of Anthony Fauci.

science reporters were not well used. Maryn McKenna, a journalism professor specializing in public health at Emory University, said major media outlets should have sent science reporters, not political reporters, to cover White House briefings during this time to increase the accuracy of reporting about COVID-19.

> "I think there's been some heroically good reporting and some really empathetic reporting as well."[1]
> —Emily Bell, founding director of the Tow Center for Digital Journalism, Columbia Journalism School

Some problems journalists faced with COVID-19 coverage are typical of all science reporting. Some stories were based on weak or nonindependent information sources, such as scientific articles that had not been reviewed by experts or drug company press releases. Some reflected uncertainty by scientists, made greater by the pandemic. Media consumers sometimes expect scientific information to be certain, and some become confused when it is not. Some scientists, including Paul Offit, the director of the Vaccine Education Center, thought the media's COVID-19 coverage was too dramatic and too negative. Finally, the pandemic was polarized and politicized from the beginning. In many cases, the news became polarized between political parties, and news stories often featured politicians more than scientists.

AMERICANS' VIEW OF THE MEDIA

Overall, the public viewed the media's coverage of the pandemic favorably, considering the public's low trust in media. A survey by the Pew Research Center in April 2020 asked a panel four questions about their response to media coverage. First, were they getting the information they needed? Second, was it accurate? Third, was the media working for the public's benefit? Fourth, was it helping the country? In all

> **THE UNITED STATES LIKES BAD NEWS?**
>
> According to a study from Dartmouth University, the coverage of the COVID-19 pandemic is much more negative in the United States than elsewhere around the world. About 87 percent of US COVID-19 coverage in 2020 was negative, compared with 51 percent in international media and 64 percent in scientific journals.[2] It was negative in both liberal-leaning and conservative-leaning media. The trend is not based on presentation of incorrect information but on which information the news source chooses to emphasize. This approach, the authors say, shades reality and may fail to clarify the truly alarming aspects of COVID-19.

cases, more people said yes than no. Margins ranged from 59 percent yes and 24 percent no on question one to 46 percent yes and 34 percent no on question four.[3] But responses were highly polarized by political party. Most Democrats approved of the media coverage, while most Republicans disapproved.

A study on newspaper and network news reporting during March through May 2020 showed that during this time, mentions of scientists in news coverage remained high and relatively stable, while mentions of politicians increased. Network news tended to focus on scientists

Sometimes, people tended to listen to politicians over health experts. Their political leaning influenced which politicians they listened to.

more than newspapers did. The study did not investigate whether the more political and polarizing news coverage affected public opinion. However, other studies have shown that such coverage encourages people to follow politicians instead of scientific experts. They may fear being ostracized by their political group unless their opinions conform to the group's. Thus, media coverage is probably helping polarize public attitudes.

HOW MEDIA COVERAGE HAS CHANGED

According to the April 2020 Pew Research poll, about 70 percent of Americans said the media has had to change the way it reports the news as a result of the COVID-19 pandemic. Democrats were about 15 percent more likely than Republicans to agree with this statement.[4] The poll did not ask how people thought the reporting had changed.

During a pandemic, public policy decisions must be based on accurate, timely information. Continually supplying this information to the public is the media's job. Media reports shape public perceptions and keep decision makers accountable. A study from the British journal *Nature* looked at COVID-19 coverage from March through

August 2020 in three countries: Canada (which had a very low incidence of COVID-19 cases), Great Britain (which had an early spike), and the United States (which had a consistently high number of cases). The study found that reporters struggled with uncertainties in information about COVID-19, such as how the disease was transmitted.

The study found that in all countries, reports from right-leaning news outlets showed lower scientific quality and often less distinction between opinion and fact. At the same time, these outlets also had less sensationalism. In contrast, left-leaning media had higher scientific accuracy but also higher sensationalism. This study wasn't the only one to note the biases in approach based on

> **DECREASING COVERAGE OF THE PANDEMIC**
>
> A study published in January 2021 showed that after a huge spike in early 2020 when the pandemic began, media coverage—measured as the number of articles in 102 high-circulation newspapers across 50 countries—decreased sharply during the year, and the decline continued into January 2021. This reduced coverage may have been due to COVID fatigue—people were just tired of hearing about it—or its preemption by other stories. The study authors felt that the media should continue to cover COVID-19, connecting it to other important challenges, such as climate change.

The way the media presents information can introduce bias, even unintentionally.

political leaning. The joint Gallup and Franklin Templeton study called Economics of Recovery found that Democrats were more likely than Republicans to understand that people without symptoms can spread COVID-19. However, Democrats were also more likely than Republicans to overstate the risks of

MEDIA COVERAGE IN DIFFERENT COUNTRIES

Two Boston University professors compared the topics of COVID-related stories in newspapers from early January through early May in China, South Korea, the United States, and the United Kingdom. Initial news stories covered scientific research, frontline health-care workers, and new outbreaks. Then, they all began concentrating more on economic consequences of the pandemic. US stories concentrated more on personal protective activities, such as social distancing and stay-at-home orders, which were often controversial topics.

COVID-19 in young people. Jonathan Rothwell, principal economist for Gallup, and Sonal Desai, an executive from Franklin Templeton, summarized the results of the study, saying, "Republicans consistently underestimate risks, while Democrats consistently overestimate them."[5] When biases such as these leak through the media, it can further hinder an effective response to a pandemic.

WHERE DOES IT END?

Since the pandemic began, people have been asking when it would be over. While the COVID-19 pandemic will likely end, with fewer people affected by it at one time, the disease is likely here to stay. It will go through changes—produce variants—but it will not disappear. People will learn to live with it. But people are still trying to figure out how to do that.

The early, optimistic view was that vaccination would solve the COVID-19 problem—that reaching herd immunity would eliminate the danger. Herd immunity occurs when a large enough percentage of the population is immune, so the disease no longer spreads. The percentage needed for herd immunity varies by disease. But vaccination rates in the United States leveled off in mid-2021, and some feared herd immunity would never be reached. COVID-19 variants such as Delta and Omicron will continue to arise, and vaccines may or may not continue to be effective against them.

As the pandemic fades and COVID-19 becomes a part of life, the media will still be responsible for keeping the public up to date on new variants, discoveries, and treatments. Unless a new and more deadly variant arises, triggering a new phase of the pandemic, news articles will become less frequent. However, the media will not forget about COVID-19. As people study the media's response to the pandemic, the results may direct the response to the next pandemic.

> ## HAPPY HOLIDAYS WITH COVID-19?
>
> During the 2021 holiday season, the COVID-19 pandemic was still ongoing. People wanted to be with their families but were worried. Public-health experts suggested the following rules: For a large, indoor gathering, make sure everyone is vaccinated and have everyone take a rapid COVID-19 test just before arrival. Have unvaccinated kids wear masks except when eating and eat separately from adults. Unvaccinated adults should wear masks to protect themselves.

CHAPTER NINE

ANTICIPATING THE NEXT PANDEMIC

Journalists around the world agree that the story of the COVID-19 pandemic has been one of the most important stories of their lifetimes. Reuters photographer Yves Herman explained: "To my knowledge, it is one of the only stories in the world, except perhaps the Second World War, which affects absolutely everyone."[1]

    The job was not easy. Journalists must go where the stories are. Often this took them into the field, where the COVID-19 pandemic was raging and where the people they interviewed may have been raging as well. As a result of antagonism toward the media, journalists describe having to remove logos from their satellite trucks and being accused of spreading fake news. Dutch television reporter Kysia Hekster said, "It is very threatening to the freedom of media, the freedom for

Reporters and journalists carried a lot of responsibility during the COVID-19 pandemic.

COLLEGE REPORTERS

The COVID-19 pandemic devasted the economy, including local news media. But one group has stepped up to produce important pandemic journalism, hold leaders accountable for safety, and even break news stories. These are college newspaper reporters. From announcing an outbreak in a college dorm to updating maps of local cases to informing the public about how school officials were withholding information about COVID-19 clusters, college newspapers were vital in keeping the public informed about the pandemic.

independent journalism and therefore also for democracy."[2]

LESSONS LEARNED

One thing members of the media have learned from the COVID-19 crisis is how to cover a crisis that they too are suffering through. The pandemic has led to editors and reporters trying to balance stories about individuals in crisis with the cold, hard facts of ever-rising death tolls—all while dealing with budget cuts, depression, relatives suffering from COVID-19, and caring for children who were learning from home. Reporters were part of the stories they wrote.

Much of the information media members needed to report on COVID-19 came from scientists, but getting that information could be a challenge. There were far too many scientific papers being released for any one journalist to read. Most science journalists try to speak

Reporters had to ensure they kept themselves safe by social distancing and wearing masks as they worked.

with scientists every day, asking which articles and topics are important enough to be shared with the public. They analyze what will be most interesting and useful to their local readers. But readers untrained in science may not be able to judge the validity of the information given. For example, sometimes scientific papers are released before they are peer reviewed, meaning before they have been read and validated by other scientists. Or a scientist with a strong viewpoint may make a statement not backed up by evidence. In either case, the information presented may be incorrect, biased, or both. The journalist must be able to catch these things before they get into print.

In May 2020, *New York Times* columnist Charlie Warzel talked about how reporters need to "embrace

LONG COVID

Fiona Lowenstein was a healthy 26-year-old when she got COVID-19 in March 2020. After her release from the hospital, she continued to suffer symptoms: gastrointestinal problems, rashes, hives, migraines, severe fatigue, and loss of the sense of smell. She had what has become known as long COVID. COVID-19 and its long-term effects were relatively unknown, so Lowenstein developed a comprehensive guide for journalists on this complication, including interviews with many patients, since symptoms vary. She cautioned journalists to acknowledge the unknown, to realize that long COVID is a chronic condition, and to remember that long COVID symptoms will outlast the pandemic.

uncertainty" when dealing with health and epidemic issues such as COVID-19. Not even health-care officials know what's going on in such a new situation, he pointed out, so what they tell reporters at first may be unclear, as with the CDC's changing guidance on the use of face masks. Such shifting messages erode trust not only in the CDC but also in the journalists. One solution, Warzel suggested, is to use "probabilistic reporting."[3] That is, admit the uncertainty and tell media consumers honestly what is known and what is not.

RECOMMENDATIONS

Reporters have sought to codify the lessons of the COVID-19 pandemic to make sure they are applied for the next time, because there will be a next time. These rules will help journalists prepare for future pandemics. One Chinese journalist interviewed several other journalists, who shared personal lessons they learned during COVID-19: Learn laws and regulations regarding infectious disease, including prevention and control policies. Check out small hospitals, not just large ones, for leads. Monitor social media. Show kindness and empathy to those you interview, and back off when necessary. Accept being turned down. And journalists should take care of themselves physically and emotionally.

A key goal for public health officials, said Dante Disparte of the Brookings Institution, will be rebuilding public trust in institutions such as the CDC, the FDA, the WHO, and pharmaceutical companies. Mistakes in their responses during the COVID-19 crisis led to distrust and unwillingness to follow their guidance. It will take time to overcome problems from this pandemic and regain this trust. Improving a worldwide early alert system to identify pandemics and listening to leaders who sound warnings would be a good start, according to Disparte. Other improvements he suggested were placing people trained in science at high levels of the federal government

STAYING CALM IN A CRISIS

Dawn Kopecki covered her first major crisis on September 11, 2001, as a young reporter at the US Capitol. Terrorists had just crashed airplanes into buildings in New York and Virginia. She remembers many details from that day—fear and horror, jammed cell phones, beautiful weather, waiting outside until 11:00 p.m. for a Congressional briefing. The day changed her life, said Kopecki, who went on to cover COVID-19. "It taught me to remain calm in the midst of crisis, helped me understand the complexities of covering catastrophic events and showed me the importance of bringing fast and accurate news to the public."[4]

and developing digital technology that can monitor threats in real time.

Andy Plump, head of research and development at Takeda Pharmaceuticals, is focused on the pharmaceutical industry's preparedness. Luck is not a pandemic strategy, he stressed, and preparing for the next pandemic must involve cooperation among global pharmaceutical companies, governments, nongovernmental organizations, and health-care systems at all levels.

THE NEXT PANDEMIC

When a new COVID-19 variant pops up, science reporter Ed Yong sees this as an audition for future pandemics. The next pandemic, he said, is already barreling toward

Some members of the media hope that the lessons learned during the COVID-19 pandemic will be remembered for the next one.

us, and we are still unprepared. "How can a country hope to stay 10 steps ahead of tomorrow's viruses when it can't stay one step ahead of today's?" he asked.[5]

The United States and the world must prepare for the next pandemic while still dealing with the first. And the media will play a crucial role. It will be the media's responsibility to make sure the public understands the truth of that crisis so people can react responsibly and without fear.

> "By getting the public on board, by giving hope, and having them realise they are part of the solution, we will succeed in beating this virus together."[6]
>
> —Leslie Rijmenams, cofounder of New6s, a Belgian association promoting constructive journalism

ESSENTIAL FACTS

KEY EVENTS

- On December 30, 2019, epidemiologist Marjorie Pollack emails ProMED-mail subscribers about an unknown virus originating in Wuhan, China.
- The Chinese government begins a campaign on January 2, 2020, to stop doctors from sharing information about the virus with the media.
- On February 1, 2020, a steep rise in news coverage of the virus begins.
- The WHO declares COVID-19 a global pandemic on March 11, 2020, triggering another wave of media coverage.
- In March 2020, clinical trials for COVID-19 vaccines begin.
- In May 2020, the disinformation documentary *Plandemic* is released.
- A January 2021 study shows that media coverage of COVID-19 decreased steadily through 2020.
- On August 25, 2021, New York governor Kathy Hochul announces that impeached governor Andrew Cuomo, whom many mainstream media outlets had praised early on in the pandemic, had underreported the total COVID-19 death toll.

KEY PEOPLE

- Ophthalmologist Li Wenliang shared concerns about a new virus on social media. He was reprimanded by the Chinese government and died of COVID-19 on February 7, 2020.
- Journalist Peter Kafka said the media should have done better at keeping the public updated without panicking people.

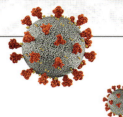

- Rhea Boyd, a pediatrician and public health advocate, cofounded The Conversation, a campaign to provide information and to correct misinformation about vaccines.

KEY STATISTICS

- By April 2020, almost 90 percent of Americans were closely following coronavirus news.
- A 2020 Gallup poll found that 60 percent of Americans have little or no trust in the media; only 40 percent showed either a great deal or a fair amount of trust. The gap is much greater by political party: 73 percent of Democrats and only 10 percent of Republicans trusted the media.
- In a Pew Research survey, 59 percent of Americans felt the media was giving them the information they needed about COVID-19.
- Social media consumption through September 2020 increased by 72 percent and posting by 43 percent.
- Only 12 individuals or organizations are responsible for 65 percent of the anti-vaccine content found on Facebook, Twitter, and Instagram.

QUOTE

"One thing that science journalists have been getting better at is not just saying what we do know, but what we don't know. But most journalists aren't accustomed to doing that."

—Laura Helmuth, editor-in-chief of *Scientific American*

GLOSSARY

algorithm
A set of steps that can be coded into a computer program to complete a process.

anti-vaxxer
A person who is opposed to all vaccines; anti-vaxxers have many different reasons for opposition, from religion to fear to mistrust of governments.

digital media
The interactive internet, enabling information transfer in both directions; social media is a large part of digital media.

disinformation
False information that is intended to harm or deceive others, often for economic or political gain.

impeached
Charged with misconduct while in office.

infodemic
A word coined by the WHO to describe an overabundance of information, some accurate and some not, making it difficult to recognize sources of trustworthy information.

lockdown
Time during COVID-19 when most businesses, schools, and more were closed and most travel was restricted to help control the spread of the virus.

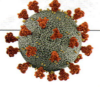

mainstream media
Traditional media including print media (newspapers, magazines) and broadcast media (radio, television) that pushes information in one direction, toward a consumer.

misinformation
False information that is created and spread but is not necessarily meant to cause harm.

mitigate
To make something less intense.

public media
Also called public service media, or PSM; media that exists to serve the public interest and benefit rather than to make a profit; usually considered more impartial than private media.

satire
A literary technique that uses humor to show that someone or something is foolish.

social media
Websites and apps that enable users to participate in social networking and to create and share content.

ADDITIONAL RESOURCES

SELECTED BIBLIOGRAPHY

Disparte, Dante. "Preparing for the Next Pandemic: Early Lessons from COVID-19." *Brookings Institute*, 16 Feb. 2021, brookings.edu. Accessed 20 Dec. 2021.

Gottfried, Jeffrey, Mason Walker, and Amy Mitchell. "Americans' Views of the News Media during the COVID-19 Outbreak." *Pew Research Center*, 8 May 2020, pewresearch.org. Accessed 20 Dec. 2021.

Head, Alison J., et al. "The Shape of the Coronavirus News Story." *Project Information Literacy*, 15 Sept. 2020, projectinfolit.org. Accessed 20 Dec. 2021.

FURTHER READINGS

Conley, Kate. *Social Media and Modern Society*. Abdo, 2022.

Edwards, Sue Bradford. *Coronavirus: The COVID-19 Pandemic*. Abdo, 2021.

Osborne, Linda Barrett. *Guardians of Liberty: Freedom of the Press and the Nature of News*. Abrams Books for Young Readers, 2020.

ONLINE RESOURCES

To learn more about the media and communications during COVID-19, please visit **abdobooklinks.com** or scan this QR code. These links are routinely monitored and updated to provide the most current information available.

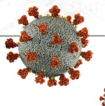

MORE INFORMATION

For more information on this subject, contact or visit the following organizations:

PUBLIC MEDIA ALLIANCE

Arts 1.80
DEV
University of East Anglia
Norwich NR4 7TJ
United Kingdom
+44-0-1603-592-335
publicmediaalliance.org

The Public Media Alliance is the largest global association of public service media organizations. It is a nonprofit organization that supports and advocates for the role of public service broadcasters in society and democracy. Public service media is highly involved in providing information on public health issues such as COVID-19.

US CENTERS FOR DISEASE CONTROL AND PREVENTION (CDC)

US Department of Health & Human Services
1600 Clifton Rd.
Atlanta, GA 30329
1-800-232-4636
cdc.gov

The CDC is a major part of the US Department of Health and Human Services. Its function is to protect Americans from health, safety, and security threats related to diseases and other health conditions and to provide information and resources regarding these conditions.

SOURCE NOTES

CHAPTER 1. THE COVID-19 STORY

1. Jane McMullen. "COVID-19: Five Days that Shaped the Outbreak." *BBC News*, 26 Jan. 2021, bbc.com. Accessed 10 Mar. 2022.
2. McMullen, "COVID-19: Five Days that Shaped the Outbreak."
3. Nectar Gan. "A Mysterious Virus Is Making China (And the Rest of Asia) Nervous. It's Not SARS, So What Is It?" *CNN Health*, 7 Jan. 2020, cnn.com. Accessed 10 Mar. 2022.
4. Sui-Lee Wee, Donald G. McNeil Jr., and Javier C. Hernández. "WHO Declares Global Emergency as Wuhan Coronavirus Spreads." *New York Times*, 30 Jan. 2020, nytimes.com. Accessed 10 Mar. 2022.
5. Peter Kafka "What Went Wrong With the Media's Coronavirus Coverage?" *Vox*, 13 Apr. 2020, vox.com. Accessed 10 Mar. 2022.
6. "Coronavirus (COVID-19) Vaccinations." *Our World in Data*, n.d., ourworldindata.org. Accessed 10 Mar. 2022.

CHAPTER 2. EARLY INFORMATION

1. Josh Margolin and James Gordon Meek. "Intelligence Report Warned of Coronavirus Crisis as Early as November: Sources." *ABC News*, 8 Apr. 2020, abcnews.go.com. Accessed 10 Mar. 2022.
2. Margolin and Meek, "Intelligence Report Warned of Coronavirus Crisis."
3. Peter Kafka. "What Went Wrong With the Media's Coronavirus Coverage?" *Vox*, 13 Apr. 2020, vox.com. Accessed 10 Mar. 2022.
4. Kafka, "What Went Wrong?"
5. Alison J. Head, Steven Braun, Margy MacMillan, Jessica Yurkofsky, and Alaina C. Bull. "The Shape of the Coronavirus News Story." *Project Information Literacy*, 15 Sept. 2020, projectinfolit.org. Accessed 10 Mar. 2022.
6. Amy Mitchell, J. Baxter Oliphant, and Elisa Shearer. "About Seven-in-Ten US Adults Say They Need to Take Breaks From COVID-19 News." *Pew Research Center*, 29 Apr. 2020, pewresearch.org. Accessed 10 Mar. 2022.

CHAPTER 3. THE MAINSTREAM MEDIA

1. Megan Brenan. "Americans Remain Distrustful of Mass Media." *Gallup*, 30 Sept. 2020, news.gallup.com. Accessed 10 Mar. 2022.
2. Andy Meek. "Fewer Americans Than Ever Before Trust the Mainstream Media." *Forbes*, 20 Feb. 2021, forbes.com. Accessed 10 Mar. 2022.
3. "Understanding the Infodemic and Misinformation in the Fight Against COVID-19." *PAHO IRIS*, n.d., iris.paho.org. Accessed 10 Mar. 2022.
4. Emily Henderson. "Study Highlights Mainstream News Media's Role in Public Health Communication during the Pandemic." *News-Medical*, 12 July 2021, news-medical.net. Accessed 10 Mar. 2022.
5. Jeffrey Gottfried, Mason Walker, and Amy Mitchell. "Americans' Views of the News Media During the COVID-19 Outbreak." *Pew Research Center*, 8 May 2020, pewresearch.org. Accessed 10 Mar. 2022.
6. Nic Newman. "COVID-19 Is Prompting More People to Head to Trusted Mainstream News Sites for Information—New Research." *Conversation*, 13 July 2021, theconversation.com. Accessed 10 Mar. 2022.
7. Saman Malik and Sarah Peterson. "How US Media Lost the Trust of the Public." *CBC News*, 28 Mar. 2021, cbc.ca. Accessed 10 Mar. 2022.
8. Newman, "COVID-19 Is Prompting More People."

9. Rachael Jolley. "Coronavirus: People Turn to Their Local News Sites in Record Numbers during Pandemic." *Conversation*, 8 Dec. 2020, theconversation.com. Accessed 10 Mar. 2022.

10. Jolley, "People Turn to Their Local News Sites."

CHAPTER 4. SOCIAL MEDIA

1. Nadim Sharif, et al. "The Positive Impact of Social Media on Health Behavior Toward the COVID-19 Pandemic in Bangladesh." *Diabetes & Metabolic Syndrome*, vol. 15, no. 5, September–October 2021, sciencedirect.com. Accessed 10 Mar. 2022

2. "The Two Sides of Social Media during COVID-19." *WARC*, 13 Oct. 2020, warc.com. Accessed 10 Mar. 2022.

3. Kathryn Buchanan, Lara B. Aknin, Shaaba Lotun, and Gillian M. Sandstrom. "Brief Exposure to Social Media during the COVID-19 Pandemic." *PLoS ONE*, vol. 16, no. 10, 13 Oct. 2021, journals.plos.org. Accessed 10 Mar. 2022.

4. Stephanie Kulke. "Social Media Contributes to Misinformation about COVID-19." *Northwestern Now*, 23 Sept. 2020, news.northwestern.edu. Accessed 10 Mar. 2022.

5. Staci L. Benoit and Rachel F. Mauldin. "The 'Anti-Vax' Movement: A Quantitative Report on Vaccine Beliefs and Knowledge across Social Media." *BMC Public Health*, vol. 21, no. 2106, 2021, bmcpublichealth.biomedcentral.com. Accessed 10 Mar. 2022.

6. Zara Abrams. "Controlling the Spread of Misinformation." *American Psychological Association*, vol. 52, no. 2, 1 Mar. 2021, apa.org. Accessed 10 Mar. 2022.

CHAPTER 5. HOW MEDIA USE CHANGED

1. Rani Molla. "Posting Less, Posting More, and Tired of It All." *Vox*, 1 Mar. 2021, vox.com. Accessed 10 Mar. 2022.

2. Suzin Wold. "COVID-19 Is Changing How, Why, and How Much We're Using Social Media." *Digital Commerce 360*, 16 Sept. 2020, digitalcommerce360.com. Accessed 10 Mar. 2022.

3. Alexandra Samet. "How the Coronavirus Is Changing US Social Media Usage." *Insider Intelligence*, 29 July 2020, emarketer.com. Accessed 10 Mar. 2022.

4. Kimberly Drake. "How Has Social Media Affected Mental Health during the Pandemic?" *Medical News Today*, 6 Oct. 2021, medicalnewstoday.com. Accessed 10 Mar. 2022.

5. Molla, "Posting Less, Posting More."

6. Wold, "COVID-19 Is Changing How, Why, and How Much."

7. Nicole Fullerton. "Instagram vs. Reality: The Pandemic's Impact on Social Media and Mental Health." *Penn Medicine News*, 29 Apr. 2021, pennmedicine.org. Accessed 10 Mar. 2022.

8. Molla, "Posting Less, Posting More."

9. Molla, "Posting Less, Posting More."

10. Ella Koeze and Nathaniel Popper. "The Virus Changed the Way We Internet." *New York Times*, 7 Apr. 2020, nytimes.com. Accessed 10 Mar. 2022.

11. "Activity on Dating Apps Has Surged during the Pandemic." *Fortune*, 12 Feb. 2021. Accessed 10 Mar. 2022.

12. Peter Suciu. "Spotting Misinformation on Social Media Is Increasingly Challenging." *Forbes*, 2 Aug. 2021, forbes.com. Accessed 10 Mar. 2022.

SOURCE NOTES CONTINUED

CHAPTER 6. THE INTRODUCTION OF COVID-19 VACCINES
1. Mark Gollom. "Why Trump's Operation Warp Speed Is Credited with Helping Race for COVID-19 Vaccine." *CBC News*, 19 Nov. 2020, cbc.ca. Accessed 10 Mar. 2022.
2. Rachel Lance. "How COVID-19 Vaccines Were Made So Quickly Without Cutting Corners." *Science News*, 29 June 2021, sciencenews.org. Accessed 10 Mar. 2022.
3. Alvin Powell. "A Public-Relations Campaign to Build Trust in COVID Vaccine?" *Harvard Gazette*, 16 Sept. 2020, news.harvard.edu. Accessed 10 Mar. 2022.
4. Desilon Daniels. "Vaccine Coverage: How—and Why—Public Media Should Get It Right." *Public Media Alliance*, 26 Mar. 2021, publicmediaalliance.org. Accessed 10 Mar. 2022.

CHAPTER 7. MEDIA BIAS
1. Marina Villeneuve. "New NY Governor Adds 12,000 Deaths to Publicized COVID Tally." *AP*, 25 Aug. 2021, apnews.com. Accessed 10 Mar. 2022.
2. Ross Barkan. "The Media's Role in the Cuomo Myth." *Columbia Journalism Review*, 18 Aug. 2021, cjr.org. Accessed 10 Mar. 2022.
3. Marian Scott. "Anti-Mask Fringe Movement Getting More Media Coverage than Warranted: Expert." *Montreal Gazette*, 29 Nov. 2020, montrealgazette.com. Accessed 10 Mar. 2022.
4. Jim Barlow. "Twitter Opposition to Face Masks Amplified by Media, Study Finds." *Around the O*, 3 May 2021, around.uoregon.edu. Accessed 10 Mar. 2022.
5. Tara Parker-Pope. "Do We Still Need to Keep Wearing Masks Outdoors?" *New York Times*, 22 Apr. 2021, nytimes.com. Accessed 10 Mar. 2022.
6. Ed Yong. "America Is Getting Unvaccinated People All Wrong." *Atlantic*, 22 July 2021, theatlantic.com. Accessed 10 Mar. 2022.
7. "Man Who Made Fun of Vaccination Efforts on Social Media Dies of COVID." *NBC News*, 24 July 2021, nbcnews.com. Accessed 10 Mar. 2022.
8. "Disinformation Dozen: Two-Thirds of Online Anti-Vaccine Content Originates From Top 12 Anti-Vax Leaders." *Cision*, 24 Mar. 2021, prnewswire.com. Accessed 10 Mar. 2022.
9. Shannon Bond. "Just 12 People Are behind Most Vaccine Hoaxes on Social Media, Research Shows." *NPR*, 14 May 2021, npr.org. Accessed 10 Mar. 2022.
10. R. Armitage. "Online 'Anti-Vax' Campaigns and COVID-19: Censorship Is Not the Solution." *Public Health*, vol. 190, Jan. 2021, pp. e29–e30, ncbi.nlm.nih.gov. Accessed 10 Mar. 2022.
11. F. Perry Wilson. "COVID and False Beliefs: How Social Media Exploits Cognitive Bias." *Medscape*, 5 May 2021, medscape.com. Accessed 10 Mar. 2022.

CHAPTER 8. FROM PANDEMIC TO PART OF LIFE

1. Jillian Mock. "'Dreck,' Drama: How US Media Handled the Pandemic." *WebMD*, 2021, webmd.com. Accessed 10 Mar. 2022.

2. David Leonhardt. "COVID Coverage by the US National Media Is an Outlier, a Study Finds." *New York Times*, 24 Mar. 2021, nytimes.com. Accessed 10 Mar. 2022.

3. Jeffrey Gottfried, Mason Walker, and Amy Mitchell. "Americans' Views of the News Media During the COVID-19 Outbreak." *Pew Research Center*, 8 May 2020, pewresearch.org. Accessed 10 Mar. 2022.

4. Mark Jurkowitz. "Most Americans Say COVID-19 Has Changed News Reporting, but Many Are Unsure How It's Affected the Industry." *Pew Research Center*, 1 May 2020, pewresearch.org. Accessed 10 Mar. 2022.

5. Jonathan Rothwell and Sonal Desai. "How Misinformation Is Distorting COVID Policies and Behaviors." *Brookings*, 22 Dec. 2020, brookings.edu. Accessed 10 Mar. 2022.

CHAPTER 9. ANTICIPATING THE NEXT PANDEMIC

1. UNRIC Brussels, "COVID-19: An Unprecedented News Story for Journalists." *United Nations*, n.d., un.org. Accessed 10 Mar. 2022.

2. UNRIC Brussels, "An Unprecedented News Story."

3. Ezra Klein. "What Should the Media Learn from the Coronavirus?" *Vox*, 1 May 2020, vox.com. Accessed 10 Mar. 2022.

4. Dawn Kopecki. "Covering 9/11 Taught Me How to Remain Calm in the Middle of Panic and Misinformation." *CNBC*, 11 Sept. 2021, cnbc.com. Accessed 10 Mar. 2022.

5. Ed Yong. "We're Already Barreling Toward the Next Pandemic." *Atlantic*, 29 Sept. 2021, theatlantic.com. Accessed 10 Mar. 2022.

6. UNRIC Brussels, "An Unprecedented News Story."

INDEX

ABC News, 47
American Public Health Association, 36
Anti-Vax Watch, 77–78

Bangladesh, 39–40
Belgium, 41–42
bias, 44, 46, 54, 65, 69, 71, 80–81, 88, 90, 95
British Broadcasting Corporation (BBC), 8
broadcast media, 20–21, 68

Center for Countering Digital Hate (CCDH), 77–78
Centers for Disease Control and Prevention, US (CDC), 13–14, 18, 21, 25, 37, 41, 52, 62, 65, 75, 96–97
China, 5–8, 10–11, 17–18, 22, 24, 40, 41, 52, 89, 97
CNN, 9, 72
college reporters, 94
confirmation bias, 54
Conversation, The, 76
COVID-19 variants, 90–91, 98
Cuomo, Andrew, 71–72

dating, 57
deaths, 7–12, 15, 21, 24, 27, 52, 56, 61, 72, 77, 91, 94
Defense Intelligence Agency, US, (DIA), 17
Democrats, 28, 30, 86–87, 89–90
digital media, 20–21
disinformation, 22–23, 25, 48, 59, 67, 76–80

Fauci, Anthony, 41
Food and Drug Administration, US, (FDA), 62, 79, 97

Gallup, 27–28, 89–90

Harmon, Stephen, 77
herd immunity, 90–91
Hochul, Kathy, 72

Idlebrook, Craig, 79
infodemic, 28

Japan, 10, 24

Kafka, Peter, 19
Kopecki, Dawn, 98

Li Wenliang, 5–8
local news, 31, 34–35, 48
lockdowns, 34, 40–41, 51–52, 57
long COVID, 96

mainstream media, 21–22, 27–28, 29, 31, 33, 34, 36–37, 73, 74
masks, 13, 18, 25, 32, 33, 37, 57, 71, 73–75, 91, 96
mental health, 40–42, 45, 52, 56
  anxiety, 35, 41–43, 52, 54
  depression, 35, 41–42, 52, 94
misinformation, 22, 25, 27, 29, 39, 43, 44, 45–48, 49, 59, 65, 67, 69, 76, 79, 83
Moderna, 61–62
MSNBC, 72

National Foundation for Infectious Diseases, 18
Netflix, 57
New York Post, 75
New York Times, 20, 33, 64, 72, 95

Operation Warp Speed, 61

Peru, 40
Pew Research Center, 25, 30, 85, 87
Pfizer, 62
Plandemic, 25
polio, 66–67
politicians, 44, 48, 71, 85–87
Pollack, Marjorie, 6, 7
print media, 20–21
Project Information Literacy, 9, 24
ProMED-mail, 6, 7
Public Media Alliance, 69
public service media (PSM), 68–69

Republicans, 28, 30, 86–87, 89–90

satire, 49
school, 12, 40, 51, 53, 55–56, 94
scientific quality, 14, 88
sensationalism, 14, 31, 88
severe acute respiratory syndrome (SARS), 5–6, 63
Singapore, 29, 40
social distancing, 40, 57, 75, 89

social media, 5–8, 15, 20–22, 25, 36, 39–40, 41, 42–45, 48, 49, 51–52, 53, 54–55, 57, 59, 73, 74, 77, 78, 81, 97
Facebook, 35, 40, 41, 44, 52–53, 58–59, 73, 78, 81
Instagram, 35, 48, 52–53, 58, 78
Snapchat, 48, 53
TikTok, 52, 57
time spent on social media, 41, 45, 51–52
Twitter, 20, 25, 45, 52, 54, 58–59, 73–74, 78–79
South Korea, 10, 89
sports, 11, 57

Taiwan, 6, 10–11
Thailand, 10, 24
Trump, Donald, 17, 24, 61, 72
trust in the media, 27–31, 33–34, 47–48, 64, 65, 69, 73, 85, 96

United Kingdom, 33–35, 49, 64, 89
Updike, Jordan, 55

vaccines, 15, 25, 41, 48–49, 57, 61–69, 71, 75–80, 83, 90–91
anti-vaxxers, 48–49, 71, 76–78, 79
myths, 65
unvaccinated, the, 76, 91
vaccine hesitancy, 15, 66–69
video calls, 51, 57
Zoom, 53, 56

Washington, 11
World Health Organization (WHO), 6–8, 9, 10–11, 18, 37, 66, 68, 97

YouTube, 41, 45, 52, 57, 73

111

ABOUT THE AUTHOR

CAROL HAND

Carol Hand has a PhD in zoology. She has taught college biology, written biology assessments, written middle and high school science curricula, and authored young-adult science books, including several on health-related topics. Currently she works as a freelance science writer.

ABOUT THE CONSULTANT

HANS SCHMIDT, PhD

Hans Schmidt received his PhD in Mass Media and Communication and his BA and MA in Communication Studies. He teaches courses in media and journalism at Penn State University Brandywine. He regularly presents his research at national and international conferences and has written more than two dozen academic journal articles, as well as book sections. He is actively involved as a member of editorial review boards, holds leadership positions with scholarly organizations, and currently coordinates the Jane E. Cooper Honors Program. Prior to his academic career, he worked as a newspaper journalist.